THE PERKS OF BLEEDING WORDS

BY AMANDA KATHERINE RICKETSON

If you think I am writing about you, you are probably right.

⌘⌘⌘⌘

WARNING

My words
may be beautiful
but my mind
is not.

PLEASE DON'T BOTHER

Don't tell me I'm beautiful
until you've seen my scars
which carve my legs
like thin white veins.

Don't tell me I'm sweet
until I've shut you out of my heart
because I swore to myself
that you are just like the rest.

Don't tell me I'm perfect
until you've seen me break down
I'll show you all the darkness
consuming my mind.

But if you
have seen my scars
bitterness
and breakdowns
then perhaps I'll believe you.

BREATHE

You are the water
I have chosen
to jump into
and the waves
are your arms
embracing me
as a I sink
like an anchor
into you.

and you are gravity
lifting me up,
so I rise from the bottom
of the ocean's depths
to dancing rays of light
reminding me
that it's okay
to resurface
and breathe.

I LEFT FLOWERS AT YOUR GRAVE

I wept for your killer
and left flowers at their grave.

If someone told me
It's impossible to
love the sinner
as much as the victim
I'd tell them they're wrong

Because when I saw your body
sprawled across the bedroom floor
with cold toes and fingers
wearing scars instead of jewels
with a bullet through your head
clasping a note that read:
"Another murder found dead"

you were still pretty damned lovely.

ANOREXIA

When I starved
my body
I tasted
the sweetest
corrupt ecstasy
of feeling thin
and beautiful

hip bones stuck
showing through skin
and it was attractive
to have a gap
between my thighs
and make every curvature
of my figure visible

and the poisonous
compliments
infiltrated my mind
and those words
were the kind of
drugs that nobody
warns you about

and this
cruel addiction
may kill me
and suffocate
the life from my lungs
but at least the
fat is gone
and I feel
pretty.

HEAVEN

Heaven is not
in your lips
because you sin
when they trace
the outlines of my body

Heaven is not
in your mind
because God
knows what
you want
when your eyes
undress me
and demons live there.

Heaven is a long way
from your heartbeat
as it aligns with mine;
it emanates
wisps of angels
to save me
from myself

and I am not
ashamed of sinning
because while
Heaven is not in you
you are my
pure, celestial
Heaven.

DEMENTOR'S KISS

and you sucked
the air out of
my lungs
(literally)
and I laughed
and told you
to do it again
and you looked at me
with the most
amused expression
and told me
I was the strangest
person
you'd ever kissed

and you did it again.

LESS AND MORE

Holding me in your arms
skin against skin
just the other night
you swore,
"nothing you can do
or say
will make me want you
any less"

and in your car
just a week later
there was nothing I could do
to make you want me
anymore.

INDIRECT HABITS

On a cold winter night
I would cling to my mother,
Tucked snugly to her right
who smelled of nicotine cigarettes.
The scent hung in our garage
in dancing silhouettes
born from a tiny tray of ash.

She'd flick her hand in a single stroke
weaving calming and nauseating
second hand smoke
into my oxygen, into my lungs
and stubbornly exclaim,
"Amanda, smoking is awful."
She'd inhale, ignite the flame,
and press the carcinogens
against trembling lips
like a smoky kiss
sighing
"Don't ever pick up
my bad habit."

Yes we are all slowly
dying
but each wisp
steals away another day
and each breath
causes her lungs to decay
school taught me in text books
smoking isn't as great as it looks

but all I saw was an easy solution
for anxiety
a horrible mental pollution
but she scolded me
when I tried the remedy myself,
"It will be your biggest regret"
she said, lighting another cigarette,
"Don't ever smoke
the habit will leave you dead
and it will leave you broke."

and I suppose that indirectly
she never meant it.

RYAN'S POEM

I asked you
in a small, quiet voice
if you had found my scars yet
and you nodded
and kissed my thighs
and left a trail of bandages
up to my mouth
and told me I was beautiful
and made me feel it, too.

GHOST TOWN

When one of my
feelings betrayed me,
frustrated and fearful,
I locked them all away
in the prison of my heart
with iron chains.
And even though
my heart is nothing
but a ghost town
at least it's still safe,
and at least it still beats.

COWARD

I keep reminding myself
that you shouldn't be
the one who got away
but you left
fleeting and slipping and howling
like the wind
and you kissed my cheek
with chapped lips
and I said nothing
and I called my heart a warrior
but I didn't even fight
all I did was build my walls thicker
but bricks and cement and guards
won't stop ghosts and
it sure as hell
didn't stop the Romans

I
am
such
a
damned
coward.

DROWNING

Loving you is like
drowning in water.

And I could save myself
if I just stood up.

SPRING

Early spring breeze
please blow me back
and carry me to ease
so my heart isn't black.

Remind me of
the way the birds awoke
 singing silly songs of love
before I used to smoke.

I am nostalgic for summer time
I crave the ocean's kiss
I'm sick of winter's clime
and the you I've come to miss.

FROST

Frost is my jailer
creeping slowly at night
into my heart, into my mind.
I'm cradled in a bleak blanket
in the height of winter's bane
when I'm vulnerable to its torture
reminding me of my past and
how my sorrows will forever last.

I shriek for my savior summer
and cry for a temporary escape.
Comforting hugs from the sun
is medicine for frostbitten scars.
The relief is merely fleeting
because now when I awake
on summer mornings with you
I am draped in daytime dew.

GIVE YOU MY HEART

I can't give you my heart
I don't care if it's broken
bruised and beaten.
I don't care if it's torn
and covered in scars.
Who cares if it's
hardly worth a penny?
And so what if
It's a mosaic of misery?

 If I lend my heart to you
there will be nothing
except emptiness
filling up my chest.

HALF OF THE TIME

Half of the time
I don't know
what I am writing about
half of the time
words spill out of me
like a clusterfuck
half of the time
I think about the rain and the sun
or about how
time has a lot of halves
but really half the time
my words
my thoughts
and my feelings
just think of you.

HEARTBEAT

you are
 beautiful as you speak
 in fragment thoughts
at (1 am 2 am 3 am)
and my emotions go
back and forth
like feet Running
ba dum. ba dum ba dum.
and I feel Terrible

but no matter how fast I flee

you are
more than the steady
beat of my heart
(which you have wrapped
in a iron-strong embrace
pulling me down to Earth
like an anchor)
you are the
ba dum [ba d]um baaadummm
          heartbeat .

of my mind

HOPE

(You're stupid.)
(What are you thinking?)
(You thought that would work.)
(Silly kid.)
(They're going to break your heart.)

I know
but I can't
give up hope
because if that light goes out
how will I find my way
back home?

(You won't)

PIECES

I am pieces of quotes
from my favorite books
stitched together by
song lyrics
and I am glued together by
midnight conversations
and the sweet taste of coffee
and I have this tendency
to fall apart suddenly

and I need you to somehow
be okay with this
because I am created by
the souls who are brave enough
to gather all my tattered pieces
and put me back together

and oh God how I would love to be whole again.

ALONE

and once again I am alone
with no one to share
songs with
and no one to narrate
how their day went
with no one
to talk to until
dreary eyes grow drowsy
and no one
to whisper
goodnight to.

MADNESS

Madness
is really strange.

It passes over me
in a whimsical blur
      I laugh
           I sing
                 I dance
but I cry myself to sleep

Madness
is pretending
you're perfectly okay

MISSING YOU

Missing you is like
walking out into the pouring rain
and expecting to stay dry.
It's like calling for peace
when the first bullet has already been shot
and it's like taking back a conversation
that you've never had before.

Missing you is needing to cry
but not having enough tears,
like screaming at night
with no one awake to hear you
and it's like loving a memory
with only ghosts to kiss you back.

It's like asking a blind man
to paint the colors of the rainbow,
or asking the deaf man
to sing you their favorite song.
It's like having a million things to say,
but saying nothing at all.

YOU ARE NOT YOUR SCARS

You are not your scars
or the blade you clasp
ever so tightly.

You are not the tears
that roll down your cheeks
like crystals.

You are not the words
you curse at yourself
when looking in the mirror.

You are a person
who got a little lost
trying to find
who they were
but instead you found
exactly who you aren't.

US AND SNOWFLAKES

It was a hurricane of snowflakes
cascading and dancing
and then falling asleep
on the ground
cuddled by icy creations
a little bit cold
and a little bit different and
a lot like themselves

And I'm thinking that maybe
you're a whole lot like me;
maybe a bit scared
and a bit confused
and maybe slightly dark
so maybe we should dance
and fall asleep
holding each other tightly,
too.

OKAY

I keep saying
I'll be okay
I'll be okay
I'll be okay
I'll be
okay
I will
be okay
I am going
to be okay
okay
okay
I will be okay
someday

but right now
I am not
okay.

ALIKE

We were so alike
that you were
more myself
than I'd like to admit.

I remember once
we both exclaimed
that "cellar door"
is the most beautiful phrase
in perfect synchronism
and it was perfect
to find an identical soul.

But then I remembered
that we both kind of hate ourselves.

NIGHTMARES

I'd rather be awake
when your memory
creeps in softly
overwhelming me
in my most beautiful
nightmares

You take
my breath away
like you did that night
when you took me
to Heaven

Your voice
resonates in my mind
sounding
an awful lullaby
I used to fall asleep to.

But when your
ghost appears
I am so ecstatic
I can hardly call it
a nightmare.

TSUNAMI

You were a tsunami
wrecking all of my bridges,
destroying all of my walls,
taking all of my breath.

I can't forget your
suffocating waves,
and I can't go back
and learn how to swim.

THEY TOLD ME TO BE BETTER

They told me to write clearer
so I took my pencil
and wrote a little more careful.
They told me to be smarter
so I took those grades
and made them all straight As.
They told me to be louder
so I took my voice
and made sure they heard it,
but then they told me to be quiet
so I sat in the back
and listened a little more closely.

They told me to be prettier
so I got some braces
and I smiled with straighter teeth.
They told me to be skinnier
so I took my food
and simply didn't eat it.
They told me to be happier
so I smiled a little more
and hid my cuts and tears.
They told me to be wiser
so I read some books
and questioned society.

Now I look myself in the mirror
and I tell myself to be better…
to be better.

But I don't know
what "better" means anymore.

SWEETNESS

I found myself
drowning
in your eyes
breathing
in your lies
instead of
oxygen.

And oh how sweet it was.

STAY

I keep thinking
of all the things I
could have said
would have said
should have said
to make you stay
to make you want
to hold on
to us.

But there was nothing
I could have done
to change your mind,
could I?

METAPHOR

Don't make me a metaphor.
I'm not a phrase of words,
or any cliché thoughts.
I don't hold the imagery
or the beauty of nature
and I sure as hell
can't compare
to kisses and coffee
or to the stars and the moon.

I am tangible
and I am real
and I can feel
Oh god, can I feel.
I walk and I talk;
I am my own entity.
I can't inspire you
or take away your pain.

I don't want to be a metaphor,
I'd rather just be me.

SNOWFLAKES

fleeting fluttering flakes
    F
        A
           L
              L
[like I did]
fastly onto
a powder blanket
of tranquil Bitterness
but even if they shiver

they are
still warmer
than you [your heart]

and they are
still colder
than me [my heart]

SUNRISE

Maybe that sunrise
didn't have the pinks
or purples
or oranges
that you wanted
but it gave you
the god damned sun,
didn't it?

WELCOME TO MY CASTLE

You said I got too close to you
and that I overwhelmed you.
You told me I relied on you too much
and I fell for you so fast

I had built my castle with many walls
but you tore them all down.
But don't worry
I stayed up all night
building them again
this time making them resistant to you
to your empty promises,
your kind words,
and all the hidden lies.
So don't worry
I won't be letting you close
anytime soon

I guess I wasn't a princess worth saving,
so next time you step in my castle
I swear to you
it's not going to be the same.

RECKLESS

I knew you would
be reckless
with my heart.

Your smile was
too sweet
and your words
too promising
and your arms
too safe.

It was reckless
to give myself to you,
but I did it anyways
with nothing to show
but a few more
damned scars.

MY DESTROYER

Who knew you would be the sun
which wakes me up every morning,
or the melodious harmony
which sings me to sleep each night?
Who knew you'd be a sea of thought
where I would drown without struggle?

You are the beat of my heart
when it's frozen with fear.
You are the breath that I take
when I can't breathe any air.
You are bones in my legs
which shatter when I fall.
You are the blood in my veins
tainted with passion and lust.

Who knew you would be
my saving grace when all was lost?
But then the demon
that drags me to Hell.
Who knew you would be
my savior and
my destroyer?

RECREATION

To create is to destroy
we build houses
but annihilate forests
we build dams
but starve ecosystems
we build cars
but taint the air.

Even creating this poem
I have destroyed
the silence in your mind.

Perhaps when we
destroy ourselves
we just want
to be recreated
as something different.

MELANCHOLY

Melancholy
hums
a dreary tune.

Sadness
drapes
over a bleak world.

Happiness
slips
through bony fingers.

Melancholy
hums
a dreary tune.

HIGH SCHOOL SUCKS

Poetry scrawled
seeps and oozes
with the
shattered hope
of
love
high school murdered.

LEAVE IT IN PIECES

Sometimes
there is no explanation
to why things
fall apart
except that the world
is an imperfect place
and even the most beautiful
and strong mountains
wear down over time
and eventually
green leaves turn red
and abandon the trees,
the flowers wilt,
grass dies,
and love breaks
and falls apart
into pieces.

We need to accept
that some things
are meant to fall apart
and it is okay
to leave those things
in pieces.

PEOPLE AND PLANETS

People are like planets
always gravitating
around someone
who is their sun.

It's sad to think
that the sun would exist
without its planets
but if the sun would disappear
they would cease to exist.

That's why people
fear the sun disappearing
and that's why people
hold on to their light source so tightly
because like the sun,
they would be fine without them.

I wonder if the sun
knows how much it affects
its planets
like how its rays
make life possible

I wonder if my sun knows
how if they were gone
I couldn't exist
the same way I did
before I met them.

OPINIONS

If you're going to give your opinion
about my hair and my clothes
or my smile or my weight,
please don't open your mouth.
I don't want opinions
on what I did wrong
because it's not my fucking job
to please you.

I don't want to hear
your opinions about me,
because when it comes to
who I am and who I will be,
the only opinion that matters
is the person staring back
when I look in the mirror.

and trust me,
her opinion isn't very nice either.

NO WORDS

Adkdjfakjd
Adjhfakdjfh
Dekdjafkd
Jdafkjdkafjd

because there
are no words
to describe
the feelings
you give me.

adkadfjkd.

MY CAT

There is nothing
more therapeutic
than waking up
after a long night of tears
and feeling a
little wet nose
hovering on your cheek
and tiny paws
 walking all over you

and I love that meow
exclaiming,
"I know you exist
and I need you
and I love you
 a whole awful lot"

(Can I have my food now?)

ENOUGH

A scar on my thigh
for never being enough
never being enough,

It's a subtle cry
I'm saying
enough is enough.
I'm sorry
I'm not enough.

I just wanted to find out
if this is what it feels like
to finally be enough.

MY DARLING STAR

Every night
I would venture outside
to visit my star
as it floated
peacefully in the night sky.
I whispered to it my hopes
my dreams
and my worries and fears.

One night
I stared outside longingly
to my dismay
I saw darkness
where my star had been.
I called out to it
but it was gone.
I wept for my star

Someone told me
that when stars die
we see them for some while
so we don't know
if a star is truly gone.

I didn't cry for my star anymore
I wrote a bittersweet letter:
it said, "Oh Darling Star
how was I supposed to save you
when you didn't even tell me
you were already long gone?"

NORTHERN STAR

You told me to be brave
but when the darkness
inside of me transformed
into demons of the night
and I stumbled along
a path that wasn't righteous
you said to look for the
northern star and told me,
"Let its light guide you home"

and when all I could hear
was your voice and I could
only feel your warmth
and I just saw the light
in your bright blue eyes
it was no wonder
I thought you were my
 northern star and pleaded,
"Please take me home"

YOUR VOICE

I can't quite
remember your voice anymore
and I think it went something like
the soft humming melody
of my favorite song,
except I can't remember the lyrics
and it is slowly getting quieter.
It stalked out like the autumn breeze
on small kitten paws
and it was such a beautiful symphony,
but now I'm forgetting it
and I'm trying to be okay with that
But I'm not.

I WAS SO DEPRESSED I FORGOT TO SIGN IT

"Why did you guys break up?"

"He didn't want me anymore."

KNIFE

You plunged a knife
into my heart
because I wanted
to be killed
and I mistook your gift
for kindness and love
and now
you have taken out
the wretched blade
and I'm still breathing
and my heart is still beating
and my bones are still aching
and it hurts
like Hell
and you're gone
and I'm
still alive.

WHEN YOU FALL IN LOVE WITH A SMOKER

Nicotine lips
kiss the sweetest
goodnight
and the scent
of smoke
clings to your jacket
and hugs me
goodbye
and lingers
sweetly diffusing
into my heart
and secondhand smoke
gathers in weary lungs
tired of breathing
and your fingers
ignite my
burnt out soul

and you are
a cigarette; carcinogens
I'd inhale for eternity
even if it kills me.

RAIN

I listened to the rain
pour onto pavement
proclaiming a dark symphony.
It cascaded from clouds
and ruptured on earth.
It was beautiful.

Then I remembered
how on that stormy twilight
you beckoned me to dance.
My hands quivered
as I lost myself in the rhythm.
It was pure serenity.

Now I stare outside
knowing that you're gone
inevitably like the lightning
only visible through
translucent, hollow memories.

Rain drops are tainted
as they foolishly collide
with the ground.

A Recipe for Pushing People Away

A table spoon of shut the world out
A pinch of don't answer text messages
Mix with being clingy and needy
2 cups of saying all the wrong things
(can substitute saying nothing at all)
Use trust issues to stir
And sprinkle in jealousy
Bake until the people you love
are gone.

WHEN I KISS YOU

When I kiss you
softly

poetry erupts
from your lips and
explodes
       into my lungs
       and fills my head
       with the silly notion
       that a love like this

might actually exist.

WATER-COLOR PAINTING

I wanted to paint
a water-color picture of us
I wanted to capture
the curves of your lips
and the swirls of colors
as they melted with mine
and I wanted to illustrate
the marks from your fingers
tracing constellations across my hips
and I thought I could draw
the way you relinquished
emptiness trapped inside of me

But I was painting a picture
with colors that didn't exist.

"WELL OKAY"

"Don't fall in love with me,"
she warned him that night.
He blinked at her and asked
"Why do you say that?"

With a huge sigh she gave her reasons,
"Sometimes I sing off pitch in the car
and sometimes my words don't make sense.
I like to watch Disney movies at home
and I talk to my cat like she's my best friend.
I write stories and poetry and read too many books
because this world frightens me so
I trip when I walk and I run into furniture
I'm really not all that great
just listen to my darkest thoughts
You'll see."

He looked at her calmly
and to her dismay
he just said
"Well, okay

What else could she say?
She couldn't plead for him to stay,
especially when she was the one
who pushed him away.

APPLE

A spherical canvas
painted with blood
the masterpiece
of passionate sinners
wielding tainted
magic
throwing you into
a dark, endless
slumber.
But what's so bad
to sleep
and be awakened
by a true love's kiss?

I WILL NOT FALL IN LOVE

He is not going to consume
my mind
my hopes, my wishes, my desires.
I won't write
silly poems about how
he's a dream
worth dreaming
and I won't talk about
his eyes
which are an essence of chocolate
I'd love to taste
and I won't mention
his lips
how they hum
a sweet Spanish song.

I won't tell you how
his smile
is a fragment of a constellation
or how he is the soundtrack
stuck on repeat
inside my head
because I don't want him
I don't want him
and I won't want him either.
He's just a boy
romanticized by
my endearing affection
and I won't be consumed
by blinding devotion.

Because if I fall for him
(which I won't)
he'll hurt my fragile soul
(which he will)
which I have guarded with
an iron austere.
So I won't fall in love
with him;
it's a reckless waste of emotion.

The only one you can count on
is yourself
because even your shadow
disappears on the darkest nights.

THE BOY WHO SAID HI

And that boy
(who I talked to because
he needed someone to listen
and I was feeling rather lonely)
told me he said "Hi" to my sister
said she looked a little bit sad and lost
and a bit angry,
and he wasn't sure why
but he asked if I
could make sure she was okay.

And then when I asked her
if she was fine
she said she was
and I didn't think anything of it.

The next day
my sister heard his name
and laughed and said,
"Why are you talking to him?
He's weird.
And not in the good way
like you and he
always says hi to me."

That was when I realized
the world can be an awful place.

YOU HAVEN'T LEFT

You never really left
at least that's what I tell myself.

I still hear you
in forgotten lullaby fragments.
I still see you
in dizzy twilight dreams.
I still feel you
in morning blanket memories.
I still smell you
in nicotine scented naptimes.
I still taste you
in coffee tainted kisses.

YET ANOTHER LOVE POEM

I'm still in love with your smile;
the way it exploded on your face
creating fissures of dimples.
It was a chain reaction
because I always smiled too

I'm still in love with your voice
whispering deep melodies
3 o clock every morning
and all throughout the day.
It was a perfect soundtrack

I'm still in love with your words
which kissed me with feelings
and put pretty thoughts in my head.
I loved the thousands of promises
all though they were too hefty to keep

I'm still in love with you
even all the parts you don't like
you were like a dream to me.
It doesn't change anything though
because you don't love me anymore.

FAREWELL

Maybe we'll meet
again in a coffee shop
nestled on a crowded street.
Maybe I'll see you and stop
to ask for your name
and we will start over again.

But for now we
did not work out.
It's painful for me
to know I'll be without
your soft whispers
rocking me to sleep.

When I said goodbye
I never intended it to mean forever
I hope someday I'll catch your eye
and we can be together

But maybe we
are just meant to fall in love
but never be together

BOOKS

A bunch of pages
clasped together by a story
constructed out of scribbled words
which comfort the mind.
it offers an artificial escape
and medication to keep you
from scratching yourself raw
and it offers a tattered friend
when abandoned by others.
In a bitter snowstorm,
it quiets nasty thoughts
fostered by reality.
It plants seeds of ideas
that bloom into flowers
creating a garden of perspective.
Long nights squinting at
white pages illuminated
by a dim light
open the mind
so it can see more.

When I was young
books gave me solace
and characters inspired me
to be a different person.
I learned to be human
devoured by darkness
because the best people
are always spawned from it.
Books were my teachers,
my friends, and my soul.

Without them I'd be long gone;
beaten by the fiction
in which we believe.
Without books
I would find
a more tragic escape
to be heard and understood
in this unforgiving world.

Pages bound together
by another author's misery
saved me a million times over
from the monsters in my head.
They bring me hope
that it is okay to be different.
If you read between the lines
of the quotes I've gathered
you would find me
in the riddles I keep hidden
from the harsh world around,
because when I underline secrets
and circle confessions
in 12 point font pages
a book won't judge me
and it keeps my thoughts safe.

Could you say all that
about your closest friend?

THE OCEAN

Enormity and
vastness swallow
sunlight
tucked in blankets of clouds;
it's a lazy late
afternoon nap

and peace
ripples in watery
tremors rocking
a lonely visitor,
but fierce
radiant light rays
keep dreary eyes
blinking.

The sun sinks
like bodies
in waves
behind the coast
and aqua lips
kiss the shore
and retreat.

Somewhere
out there
someone is drowning.

WHEN A TEACHER MADE ME WRITE HAIKUS:

Words roll off your tongue
and they are not poetic
but you won't shut up.

It is cold outside
the cars aren't nice to look at
and I'm fucking cold.

There is not beauty
in wilting, sienna grass
and tainted brown snow.

The sun is a tease
promising to bring summer
but I still see snow.

It's morbidly cruel
when nature begs for a drink
and is killed with snow.

A genius will go
outside, look around and say:
"It's not that pretty."

ESCAPE

Sometimes I escape
the ugliness of my mind
when I inhale your breath
and wrap myself in your arms.

I liked to escape this world, once
by carving self inflicted scars
and starving myself
until I'm the perfect size.

And that escape used to numb me
so the pain fled my soul,
leaving me with empty nothingness
and sang me a tempting melody.

But when you kiss my scars
and run your fingers down my spine
whispering about how I might not be perfect
but I am perfect for you

I find I have stumbled upon
a sort-of Heaven with you.

SHE DID NOT SMILE THAT DAY

There was a little child
who picked flowers in the garden
and cried when the dandelions were sprayed.
I remember holding her in my arms,
witnessing her laugh about nothing
and smile
just because the stars glowed at night.

There was a growing girl
who collected books on a shelf
and loved them because they didn't mock her.
I remember her coming home
and wiping away the tears
but smile
because she didn't want me to see.

There was a young woman
who withheld feelings inside
but starved and slashed her body.
I held her hand that day
as she revealed how unhappy she was.
She didn't smile
because she didn't think she'd be okay.

DEMONS

You told me
a tale of monsters.
You read me stories
of faraway places
and encouraged
me to create
a whole new reality.

I shrieked as playfully
you scared me,
spinning a story
of how the house across the ditch
is haunted by malevolent demons.
I walked there one day
and found nothing there.

I kept looking for
the darkness you spoke of.
I wanted to find a world
more exciting than this.
I wanted to find monsters
that made people seem friendly.

Eleven years later
I found where the
demons hid.
I found out how
they were created.

They have been with me all along.
Silly father,
demons don't live in house or stories or faraway lands.
They live inside my head.

ACID RAIN

If your love was the rain;
toxic pouring from gray skies,
I'd hold out my tongue
and collect all your acid lies.

THE POINT

What's the point of talking
when nobody bothers listening?
What's the point of hurting
when no one is here for comforting?
What's the point of staying
when you only taught me leaving?
What's the point of screaming
when people are always quieting?
What's the point of asking
when a ghost is only answering?

What's the point of living
when they only care about existing?
But what's the point of dying
when you can't see all the caring?

LIED TO

I have been
lied to
and they
say lying
is wrong
but the star
falling to
its death the night
I met you
fooled me into
thinking
I was lucky enough
to have something
that was never
meant to be mine.

SONGS

Today I heard
that song you used to hum
on the radio
and I almost sung along
but I bit my tongue.
I remembered every note
and every shift in the melody.

Oh how I loved that song,
that little piece of you,
and when you left
I locked that song away
to keep it from luring my heart
with ghostly memories.

Now I can't
help but wonder about
what songs you are
singing to her,
and if your reusing the
same wretched love songs.

I hope you know it's fucked up
to keep ruining songs for people.

STARS

and if I
could grab
the stars
by their hands
and dance across
the constellations
and the milky darkness
I swear
they couldn't hold me
as well as you.

ARTIFICIAL LIGHTS

Little lights
hung and
twinkled above us
like stars
and the light danced
over plush green grass
and my skin
kissed the blades
while you
kissed my heart

and you pointed
at the sky, at the
valiant artificial stars
and declared,
"I want lights like that
on our porch someday."

CAREFUL LOVE

I don't want
to love you
recklessly
like the wind
loves the dirt
and the leaves
and dances with the trees.

I want
to love you
carefully
like the rain
loves the grass
and the rivers
and shares kisses with the flowers.

HEARTACHE

You spent so long
wondering
and asking
"How can anyone love me?"
and you counted your flaws
but didn't have
any fingers left
for strengths

and when someone finally
said they loved you
all you could ask
was "Why?"

instead of telling them
that you loved them, too

IF YOU ASK ABOUT MY NAME

Amanda Katherine Ricketson
Nine syllables.
Twenty five letters.
It means a lot of things
to different people.

I never loved my first name
I heard "Amanda Please" endlessly,
and of course,
"uh man duh"
sounded out to ridicule me.
But then some boy,
who loved too carelessly
taught me my name
meant love.

Once I wanted to change the spelling
of my middle name
to "Cathryn"
after my favorite author.
Books spoke to me when friends didn't,
they showed me sorrows
that were too real to see,
but I learned Katherine is the name
of my father's mother;
she killed herself before he was three.

My last name belongs to my dad.
Word always corrects it
to "rickets on"
which is a childhood disease.
I am indifferent about it, but
it marks where I come from
but not where I will go,
Because someday a boy
will come along and change it.

I wonder what you think of
when you say my name
all nine syllables
and twenty five letters.
I sure hope
you think of better things than me.

EPILOGUE

I am so sorry for anyone who relates to my poetry or is hurt by seeing the darkness in my mind. This is for all the boys who have broken my heart and the boys who have taught me I shouldn't be afraid to love again. It is for the people who have shaped me and the people who have told me I am not good enough and that I can't make it. Also, it is for the people who are telling me to better and the people who tell me I am perfect but show me otherwise. It is for the friends who have left me and the friends who stand by my side even when I push them away. It is dedicated to the ghostly memories, nostalgia for the past, and the terrifying realization that the future is fast approaching.

It has been a long year since writing all these poems and cheers to another year writing more poems to live with reality.

When people ask me how I learned to write I simply tell them this: "There is nothing to writing, all you do is sit at a typewriter and bleed." Ernest Hemmingway.

Amanda Katherine Ricketson

ABOUT THE AUTHOR

Amanda Katherine Ricketson, also known as AKR, is a 17 year old from Windsor, Colorado. Growing up in a small town has proved to be difficult, but she spends a lot of time with her friends and family. She is a senior in high school with aspirations of becoming an author. She is an avid blogger on tumblr.com and that is where she discovered her talent and love for poetry.

Made in the USA
Lexington, KY
18 November 2017